The Autobiography of Patsy McNeil

BY PATSY MCNEIL

Dedication

To My Family

As barefoot girl from Church Creek, Maryland, I crawled across the plowed ground, planting and picking tomatoes, cucumbers and string beans. We also husked corn. The field was so big and long. There were acres and acres of land. On the farm we had horses, cows, bulls, pigs, chickens and ducks.

The farm was located on Maple Dam Road. My father, James Banks, and my mother, Rita Banks, had fourteen children. My parents were sweet and loving people. They believed in the gathering of family. To this day I can still remember the brown lunch bags we took to school. I remember the little radio we had. All that radio played was country music. We listened to Hank Williams, Ernest Tubbs and Lefty Frizzell. I loved country music and still enjoy hearing it to this day. I also loved singing hymns. As a little girl I prayed to Jesus this prayer, "When I get older I want to marry a singer."

Jesus answered my prayers. My first husband was indeed a singer, but after eight years of marriage, that relationship ended in divorce. When it ended, I was living in a town called Cambridge, Maryland. With only a high school

education, I began to look for work. I was hired at a local crab house, then a tomato factory, then a garment factory. I was living check to check and could hardly make ends meet.

Somewhere along the way, I'd heard of a city named Trenton, New Jersey. I heard that jobs were plentiful; lots of good jobs. So one day, in 1966, I made up my mind that I was going to go there, and that's just what I did. When I got to Trenton, I found a job working at the Circle F.

There, we manufactured parts for electrical use: electric sockets, surge protectors and night lights. Up to that point in my life, that was the best money I'd ever made. Next, I found a row house. My family and I were all together as one big happy family. Experience has taught me is this one thing that: What Jesus has for you is for you! I know that for sure; can't nobody take it from you!

As the years went by, I met and married Henry McNeil. We found a church and fell in love with Jesus. Then, more years passed and the spirit of prayer became a part of my life. I found the need to just pray, pray, pray. I would pray for people everywhere and especially liked to pray that Jesus help people in need.

My years in Trenton, New Jersey were the best years of my life. We always had family

gatherings; I had a good job and a husband to join me in my walk with Christ. I loved those eighteen years in Trenton, but it was in my heart to go home again. In 1983, my husband and I moved back down south to the town of Salisbury, Maryland.

Let me tell you, no matter how long you have been in a place, if you feel in your spirit that it's time to move, I pray that you move! I am writing this book to let people know if God be for you, it is more than the whole world against you.

The house that we would live in had been built a year earlier, in 1982. We moved to Salis-

bury with no jobs, but we were not worried about how we were going to make it. We knew that Jesus cares and provides. Weeks went by, and guess what? We both found jobs. The pay wages in Salisbury were so low, but we made it anyway. One day, in 1987, the Lord put it in my heart to open my own business. Jesus said, 'If you can go from house to house taking care of people, why don't you put in your own house.' I replied to the Lord, 'I don't know how to do that.' Jesus never said nothing else. So we went to Kmart and my husband bought a file cabinet and in three years, I had five clients. That was nobody but Jesus. Jesus did that. One thing I always do is pay tithes in my church.

FOR THOSE OF YOU WHO WANT YOUR OWN BUSINESS SAY THIS PRAYER

Father, In the name of Jesus, I thank you so much for what you have done for me. And what you have done for me, you can do for anyone that needs and wants to go into their own business. Open up a door for them. I pray in Jesus name, Amen.

NOW AS YOU SAY THIS PRAYER,
BELIEVE AND YOU SHALL RECEIVE.

In 1989, I wanted to get a medical transportation vehicle to take people to hospitals, nursing homes and day centers for the elderly. In order to do it, the state sent me this huge application packet to read over and fill out. I said to my husband, "There is no way I can fill out these papers!" So I asked Jesus, 'Who I can get to help me do these papers?' Jesus told me the name of a person to call. So my husband called him immediately, the man picked up and said, "Bring the papers to me right away." A few days later he had them filled out. He was such a loving person. Still, I had a few more pages that needed to be filled out. So I said to Jesus, "Where can I take these papers?"

So plainly, he told me the place to take them and that's where I went. The young man was reading over the papers and I felt the need to pray. He acted like he was not going to sign them. But then, as I prayed he began to sign them. I felt a turnaround as the man signed those papers. He had to sign those papers because we were sent there by Jesus. I thanked the

young man and the next day I went to Motor Vehicle and I was on the road in another business.

I write to all of you to let you know that I am not most educated person. I only went to high school, but what I did do, was Jesus doing it through me. God is able to do exceedingly and abundantly above all that we can ask for or think according to the power that is working within us. Jesus is still blessing me. For years I had a food pantry giving food to those in need. I loved what I was doing. Whatever Jesus tells you to do I pray that you do it. You will be blessed in many ways.

Prayers

and

Hymns

— *1* —

I feel the need to pray for those that are sick, in hospitals, nursing homes, in their own homes or wherever they may be. Jesus you see and know all things. You see those that are sick and feel like they just can't go on; but I know you are a healer. You can heal all kinds of diseases and you said in your Word, by your strips we are healed. You said many are the afflictions of the righteous but the Lord thy God will deliver. You sent your word, and I believe, they are all healed in your holy name. Amen.

— 2 —

I feel the need in my spirit to sing:
When we all get to heaven,
What a day of rejoicing that will be.
When we all see Jesus,
We'll shout the victory.

— *3* —

I've been trying to finish this book for many years. So today I ask Jesus to anoint this book so it will bless and encourage thousands of people all over the world to get to what Jesus has for them because what is for you is for you. Nobody can take it from you.

— 4 —

I feel the need to pray again for all young men who have been hurt. You feel like nobody cares. Your daddy has not been in your life like you wanted him to be. I want you to know you have a Heavenly Father that loves you so much that he bled and died on the cross for you. And he said in the Bible, John 15: 7, "If ye abide in me, and my words abide in you, ye shall ask what ye will, and it shall be done."

— 5 —

I feel this hymn in my spirit:
Yes, Jesus loves me,
This I know,
For the Bible tells me so.

— 6 —

I feel the need to pray again and ask that Jesus anoint this book that whoever reads it shall be blessed coming and going out. Pressed down, sharpen together and running over.

— 7 —

For the young lady who is working to take care of your children, and the Fathers are not there to help you, Lord Jesus, give them the strength they need to do all that they need to do, and let them know they are going to be alright, and their needs shall be shall be met. Just put God first in their lives. I was young and now I am old, yet I have never seen the righteous forsaken, nor seed beg for bread. You just thank God for Jesus Christ, the Son of the living God!

I want to thank you God for all of my family. I want to thank you for supplying all of the people, over the years, who helped me take care of my clients. I want to thank you for all of the other jobs you have helped me with because I could not do it by myself. I am getting up in age now, and I am still in business. With family standing by my side, I want to encourage your heart as you read this: Be strong in the Lord and always put God first and all things will fall into place.

There have been people who have asked me, "How do you do what you do?" I always say it is Jesus. The anointing of God is upon me, and I can do all things through Christ who strengthens me. There have been many days that I had to pray three times a day or more, for myself and my clients. Jesus has always come through for me because when you care for others you need to take time to care for yourself. Don't think it's easy. There have been times when I had to stop, look around, and see how in the world I wiped clean all that was on my plate in one day. Jesus gave me strength and I have to stop and give Him a hallelujah praise.

— 8 —

Hallelujah, hallelujah,
THANK YOU, JESUS.

— 9 —

What a friend we have in Jesus,
All our sins and grieves to bear!
What a privilege it is to carry
Everything to God in prayer!
Oh what peace we forfeit,
Oh what needless pain we bear,
All because we do not carry
Everything to God in prayer.

Before I end this book, I want you to know that I am the Mother of five sons and one adopted son. I have two beautiful daughters. I have twenty-five grandchildren, numerous great and great-great grandchildren. God has been more than good to me and my family.

Let me pray for my family.

—

Father, I come in the Holy Name of Jesus to thank you for letting me see another day to pray for my family and our world. Let the family love one another. Forgive one another. Comfort one another. Help one another. Don't get into groups and love only the part of your family. But love all of your family. If you don't have love, ask Jesus for it. He already knows what you need. In Jesus name, LOVE. Amen.

I started my life as a little girl crawling across the plowed grounds of Church Creek, Maryland. I am still on my knees to this day praying to God, praising God and thanking God.

www.ingramcontent.com/pod-product-compliance
Lightning Source LLC
Chambersburg PA
CBHW040316050426
42452CB00018B/2868